8 AUGUST

franciszka
voeltz

8 August ©2019 by **Franciszka Voeltz**. Published in the United States by Vegetarian Alcoholic Press. Not one part of this work may be produced in any way without expressed written consent from the author. For more information, contact vegalpress@gmail.com

Cover art and illustrations by Corinne Teed

8 august

2009	3
2010	9
2011	15
2012	21
2013	29
2014	33
2015	39
2016	47
2017	53
2018	57

8 AUGUST 2009
MÉTIS, QUÉBEC

grieving you while you are still here

our bodies suspended
in the netting of an oversized
multi-human hammock
we sway weightless
over the herb garden
and pluck the mint
holding its green sprigs
to our upper lips and showing off
our aromatic mintstaches

―――――

hijacked lupine seed pods
stowed away
in back jeanskirt pocket

―――――

an art installation
collection of mini cabins
one featuring shelf after shelf
of water-filled mason jars
another two layer moment:
the first being the right here right now,
the second layer being
if the dream was still ours,
we'd laugh giddy

about a glam-rock wedding here
commitments spoken
among mason jars
and walls of paper tacked up
to be written on
little cabins to disappear into
to make out in
to hold the stories of us

———

scones
scrambled eggs
strawberry jam
front porch sun
wheat bombed stomachs
weighing us down

———

le jardin's green
oversized adirondack chair
everyone takes photos here
including ash and i
our feet swinging high off the ground
our shoulders and arms summer-tan

———

afloat in the chill of sea salt
body carried by waves
little mini shrimps nibbling at my limbs
how i am held here
how the world goes weightless
how the medicine
of cold shock against skin
is baptism out of this body
out of this deep-lodged ache
out of this broken raw broken open

———

theory's golden body
swimfloating and paddling
with huge branch in happy mouth
bobbing freshwater saltwater swirls

———

four more days until i'm eastward-
bound
leaving behind the grieving-you-while-
you-are-still-here
to be carried off on the currents
of the st. lawrence/
fleuve saint-laurent

8 AUGUST 2010
VANCOUVER, BRITISH COLUMBIA

wrestling fig trees with a blackberry bramble and a gold belt

wrist-splinted max
talks about rigging up a bike
for one-handed operation
while i slice dried figs
and corinne slices tomatoes thin
and soula tends to the frittata

———

awake/not awake
vancouver water in my neti pot
they say that smell is the sense
most strongly linked to memory

———

wrestling fig trees
with a blackberry bramble
and a gold belt
the three of us
plus two women from the
neighborhood
(simultaneously cheering us on
and telling us to be careful)
bring the ripe red insides
to our mouths

———

soula leads us through the largest
community garden in canada
takes us to the quince tree
and makes us guess the fruit
which is ripe in late september
when it turns bright yellow
and loses its fuzz

———

main and first
around the corner
from the pacific central sign
perched over the old train station
we walk over the heat
of fresh-pressed blacktop
moving faster than the backed-up traffic

———

soula explains
that because vancouver is a port city
a lot of things get brought in
and left here
like heroin

like crack
like cocaine

———

corinne tucking honeymoon flowers
from the mythical land
behind her ear
along the train tracks
in other worlds
these flowers are known as
pearly everlasting

———

three mason jars of cold water
on blackpink formica table
at the foundation
where i am an overlay
of past and current selves
amorous
bewitched
splintered
whole/healed

———

rainbow aqua busses
moving slow along the water
science world to our right
the curve of metal
holding us up
eyes closed
i am not sleeping
i am filleting you

———

two stories
from two cities
in one day
about tossing furniture
from balconies and third floors
roll top desks
and a baby grand

———

your name
is more
than holy

8 AUGUST 2011
SAN DIEGO, CALIFORNIA

twining me twice back

i'm pretty sure i dreamt
about that ocean water
but even if not
i certainly fell asleep and woke up
with a filmstrip of waves rolling
in my head

―――――

front teeth scraping
pulp from skin
the imbalance of sour/sweet a sign
that citrus season has passed

―――――

kaya kitchen-sitting
in a mini lumberjack-print vest
and bright blue stocking cap
arm rigged up in biketube sling
your curls!
she says
ocean hair!
i respond

―――――

radio station
two doors down
at the house under construction
plays my high school days
greatest hits
starting with
love buzz by nirvana,
and *fade into you* by mazzy star
and ending with
here comes your man by the pixies

———

two silver pots on stove
water beginning to boil while i
wash a sinkful of green grolsch bottles

———

four teaspoons of rose petal black tea
crammed into a linen tea bag
bouyant pouch bobbing
in steaming water

———

i build an egg stack lunch with
kaya's home-made biscuits

vegenaise
garden tomatoes
garden basil
and a sprinkle of salt

———

listening to npr
i miss the name of the clause
but they talk about how during world
war two, the clause sent upwards of
15,000 people (most presumed to be
gay [lesbian/queer/trans])
to death camps
and even though i knew
of the pink triangles and their origins
it isn't until now i realize
the double braid twining me twice back
to the seeds of struggle and the
gut-deep hunger
for liberation of all humans
(and sentient beings)

———

slicing red-leaf lettuce with an almost
sharp knife
while the nina simone mixed tape gift

(a la tyler sledge) plays
how i could rewind and listen
a million times
to the sequence of her covers of
suzanne,
who knows where the time goes
and *to love somebody*

———

perhaps the most important item
to pack for the journey:
the gold sequined short shorts
which i zip into backpack sidepocket

8 AUGUST 2012
MARQUETTE, NEBRASKA

adorno is me / i am adorno

driving south on the 14
corn on one side
soy beans on the other
of note:
the *crooked creek gun club* sign
to our right

———

olivia in the front seat
and av at the wheel
driving through the bunkers and
mounds of the naval ammunition depot
in hastings, nebraska featuring 49,000
acres of munitions plant and storage
av tells us of the cahokia mounds - site
of the largest known ancient indigenous
city/earthworks mounds (A.D. 700 to
1400) north of Mexico named for the
cahokia subtribe of the illiniwek
10 miles east of modern-day st. louis,
and she tells us of the milam landfill
built two miles from cahokia
with indignance
says something
about how the only mounds in the u.s.

that seem to matter
are these: military and trash

———

in this truck
av talks about the possibility
of poetry after auschwitz
referring to that adorno quote:
poetry after auschwitz is barbaric/
there is no poetry after auschwitz
the shock and resonance that follow
every time i hear this quote that
i formulated and spoke before i ever
read it is proof
that time is not linear
(adorno is me / i am adorno)

———

at some point
we substitute sound for words and
serenade the road, the corn, ourselves
with maria callas cranked up
truck cab wind in my hair
something about how place receives
sound
(calla's voice landing

in the gold dried tassels)
or something about how sound
augments place
(callas's lilt drawing out the gentle rise
and fall of the fields)
perhaps it's how her voice gives shape
to the sorrow of my own chant:
the buffalo, the buffalo,
once the buffalo...

———

and under all these dried husks
i acknowledge you, oglalla aquifer
largest in the world
lying under the great plains
your core within the borders
of this very state
how 3,500,000,000 billion acre-feet of
water percolated into you over
hundreds of millions of years
and since we've begun tapping into you
in the 1950's for irrigation,
you have dropped 253,000,000 million
acre-feet
and i hear every year now
more wells on the edges of you

have begun pumping sand
instead of water

———

the kindest 30-something woman
in a yellow shirt standing behind the
newly opened coffeeshop/bookstore
counter apologizing for only having one
slice of pie left which is enough for the
three of us to split (and give the extra
bites to olivia, the birthday queen)
the slice of pie over which i
talk about how fucked up it is
that everything about the willa cather
tour/video we watched
overlooks her longtime women
companions and
disregards the fact
that she (in her high school years)
often went by *william* and
wore her hair shaved/shorn
accented with ties and other
'mens' wear

———

and on the way back
we ride over the west fork of blue river
in clay county

and i can tell there is water
before we roll over it
because the tree line
in all this flatness
gives it away

———

spirits coming alive
in the form of night wind
churning up what was quiet prairie
into the rustling of green things
and drought-dry things
against one another

8 AUGUST 2013
IOWA CITY, IOWA

balance beaming

like a card in the bottles suit of the
collective tarot i say
about my morning halfsleep while the
kitchen sounds of
blueberry pie-making
seep in

―――――

balance beaming on a concrete parking
lot slab outside a thrift store named
crowded closet
man calls out from the sidewalk
i like your tattoos
while shiz talks
on the other end of the phone line

―――――

soaked nuts, skinless
is one way to describe it we joke
regarding the crust of the raw vegan
blueberry pie
pressed into the pan

―――――

pockets of the world corinne says on the
green couch
is my favorite food
(empanadas, samosas, pierogies,
dumplings etc.)

―――――

two mosquito bites
one on the back of each calf
inside the gates of natalie and vanessa's
garden

———

it's not only about water
(*patagonia rising,* a film about a
proposed five-dam project in patagonia)
it's about the faces of the people
who tell their water stories

———

warm light radiating
behind a yellow lampshade
next to a bed in a room that isn't mine
but feels easily inhabitable

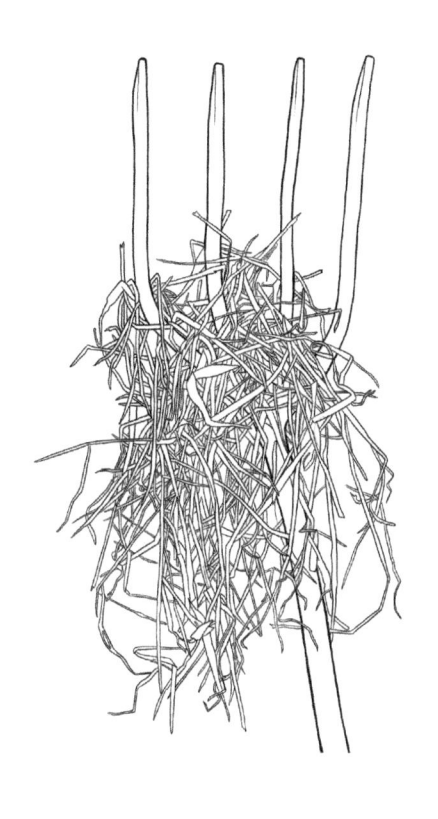

8 AUGUST 2014
RUTLEDGE, MISSOURI

in the uprooting

a bell for tea-time and a
bell for the tour
and later trish explains
that in chinese medicine
one cannot get so much as even a drop
of rain on their heads
and the reason the young teen
wouldn't take a seat at the
work party because she wasn't
supposed to be cleaning potatoes
while bleeding

———

found in the uprooting:
a spider that looks like it could
do some damage and a small
brown/dark brown snake
that looks like it couldn't

———

raincoated and tshirted kids
in the brassicas
marveling at how the leaves
hold the water
they bend down to sip
along the leaf-spines
and slide their muddy dirt-hands
over to wash

———

little bits of life
landing on me
is how i talk about
how good it feels to be
working in the
drizzly almost-rain
(feeding my part-pacific-northwest
spirit)

———

six carts of
hay separated from its
decomposing bale
pulled from one end of south garden
to the other
and lifted with a pitchfork
one clump at a time
to mulch the once-upon-a-time
cabbage beds

———

the puff of
what looks like steam but is
more like mold-dust
rising out of hay clumps
we pull apart

———

if i didn't know you
and you were coming here for a visit
and i asked you if you thought this
bread was store-bought

what would you say
emory asks his mom about the
store-bought looking round loaf
that mica made with sifted sandhill flour
which does indeed look
bakery-made and bought

———

*i've had some zuccanoes
in my day* i tell trish while
motioning to my plate
*but these
these are it*

———

in absence of a respirator
i tie a light lavender bandana over my
mouth and nose so i can take a seat
at my desk in the loft
where the mouse shit-smell permeates

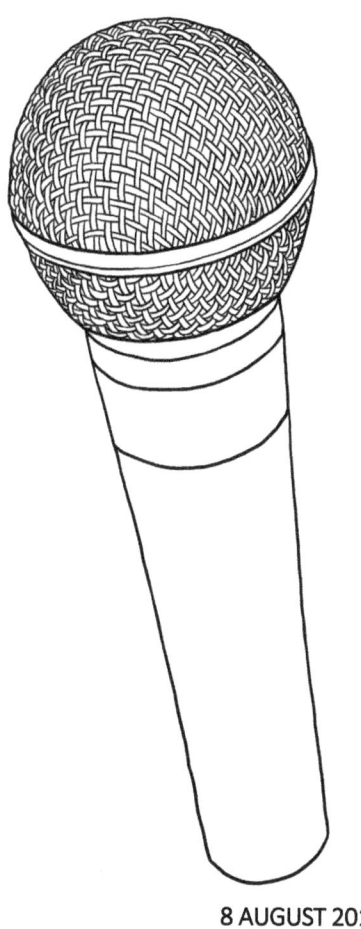

8 AUGUST 2015
RUTLEDGE, MISSOURI

our lungs at work

i'm holding the gem of us
and the work/idea/plan/hope
is to keep my eye on its gleam
cutting through all the other noise
banging to get in i say leaning
on forearms on butcher block

---

we laugh about the thought of
(welcome to) *fist city* knuckle tatts
as honna pits some damson plums and i
scrape cucumber seeds from flesh
fist city as in *knuckle sandwich*
fist city as in the shape one can take
curled up inside another

---

manila folder of writing workshop magic
word scraps spilling out aflutter
from ceiling fan circulations
onto couch cushion between
honna and i as we write
in our lap-perched notebooks

---

written in aforementioned notebook:
somewhere i was taught
that land doesn't migrate
only its creatures do
movement- swift as a river re-routing

*slow as the bones we are made of
giving themselves back to soil*

*i began at the water's edge
which is always shifting
meaning the exact point can't be pinned
same as where we were
when we first dreamt us
and by us i mean
where you first dreamt you
and i first dreamt me and
each of us first dreamt we*

*there is a picture of our pairs of feet
in zig-zaggy patterned socks
 and two-tone boots
at the edge of the rolling rio grande
same edge now submerged
under the rise of
summer's excessive stormings*

*the shape of the lake i was born next to
(michigan)
is not the same shape it was
39 years ago
not the same shape it was last week*

―――――

new information i say
in the back seat to mica

it takes a while to sink in
and we segue into singing a round of
when i was young
i was the sun
shining through the trees
onto the ground
when i was young
i was a mountain....

———

and now for something completely
different i joke
about taking the back way
to dancing rabbit which
looks not completely different at all
from the front way

———

little collisions of kale and i
in path of the frisbee
our faces red our lungs
at work
the cold pond waiting
to cool our sweat-skin
when the game is done

———

honna, mica, emory and i
howling *whoah-oh we're halfway there*
oh-oh! livin on a prayer
out sedan windows as we roll
up the gravel drive

———

living room karaoke we
pass the mic around the couches
in our costumery opening with
livin on a prayer and closing with
stand by me/blue moon
and middled with tyler
singing *achy breaky heart*
(tell your brother Cliff whose fist can tell my lip
He never really liked me anyway)
and that cheeseburger song

———

trish's skirt as disco ball
casting sequin shimmers
onto the ceiling
from the beam of honna's mini
projector that shines lyrics onto the
thumbtacked sheet
dangling between living room and
dining room

———

the magic of a microphone - we joke
about having one at all times
calling out across the kitchen circle
or out in the potato fields *you! love you!*
like a standup comedian
talking to the

half-empty din

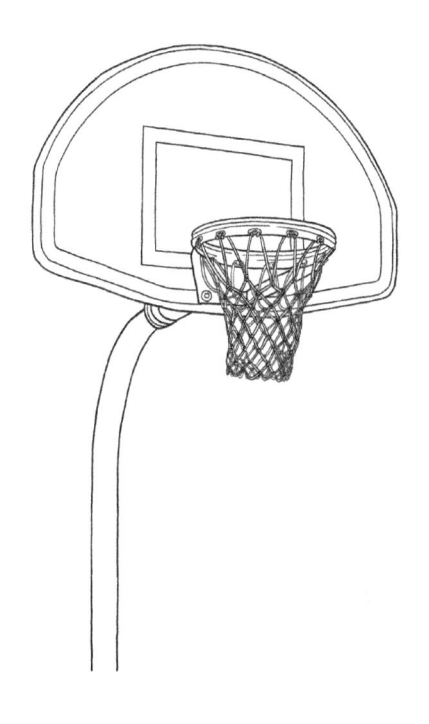

8 AUGUST 2016
RUTLEDGE, MISSOURI

the long legs of the distance animal

every day it's a gettin closer
going faster than a roller coaster
weeds like these will
surely go away
i sing in the asparagus patch
where the crew of us works our way through
tugging at and forking up the lamb's quarters, the smartweed, the velvet leaf, the shepherd's purse, the chicory, (some of which stand taller than us)
that, when piled together,
tower in piles at least seven feet

———

we move down the beds
plucking edamame,
only the plump-beaned pods
that plunk plunk into our five gallon buckets
and then up/down the lookfar tomato weeds and then
up/down the brassica leaves
all the while trading updates
of people and place

———

the okra leaves
touching/brushing my back

as i crouch under to lean in
to the parsley that i cut
with my favorite knife
whose blade curves
like a J

———

sadness is a gift
to closeness mo says
as i lean into the soft deep grief
which i follow by naming trees:
american persimmon
siberian elm
red maple

———

the long legs of the
distance animal mo drew
on a white piece of paper that she
gifts me

———

style! we keep calling
on the b-ball court (also known
as a gravel driveway)
while incorporating things like
sticky-outy elbows and handstands
and moonwalking
into our technique

———

the parchment/gold glow
of the almost-half-moon

reflected on the clear plexiglass
of the basketball hoop backboard

———

the braided rope (hammock) marks
pressed
into liana's shoulder blades
and the back of sancho's arms

———

the un-funny jokes we read
around the butcher block from
emory's piñata-score laffy taffy
wrappers

———

the single leaf of sage
whose edge glows red
and whose smoke i weave around
the cards
my body
the bottoms of my bare feet
the doorway

8 AUGUST 2017
RUTLEDGE, MISSOURI

for imaginary explosions

the meditative repetition
of bringing canful by canful of water
to the young chinese cabbage,
the purple fall cabbage,
the asters, the zinnias, the dahlias,
bachelor's buttons, cockscomb,
globe amaranth and snapdragons
while, just feet away,
a crew of frenzied kids shout names for
their invisible war vessels
and scream for backup by the swing set
firing fake bullets and
kerblamming out the sounds
of imaginary explosions

———

still-warm-from-the-dehydrator-trays,
the sun-dried sungold tomatoes
i pass one by one
into henri's (age two) reaching hand

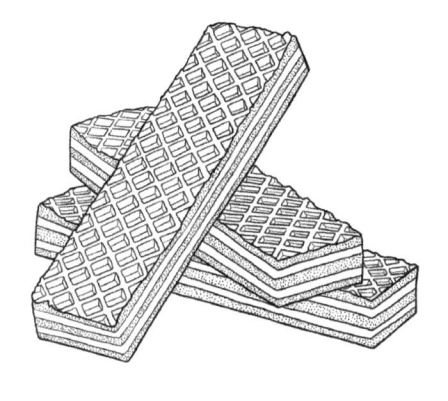

8 AUGUST 2018
VIROQUA, WISCONSIN

a litany of improv insults

on the gravel shoulder
bike-riding home
i curse and growl and grumble and roar
mostly about gender
mostly about what it's like to be stuck in
a situation where basic respect towards
(you name it:
people of color
jewish people
people with physical and/or mental
disabilities
women
people of size
etc.)
is so lacking in several male-socialized
co-workers
that i am stunned

so picture me
pedaling along shoulder
of a 55 mph highway
pedaling and sweating and spitting
as i call to the wind,
as i call the problematic men
problematic phrases starting with *pig*
but i love pigs
so i indulge

in a litany of improv insults including
fuck you, you fuckin' turducken
which then makes me laugh out loud
in the bright sun alongside the fast cars
passing
so i call it out again
fuck you, you fuckin' turducken!!!
grinning as i grit my teeth
up the steep gravel hill

―――――

the flavor of gluten-free lemon wafers
that neither of us can name
until jennifer says fruit loops
which is exactly it

GRATITUDES:
freddy la force and corinne teed especially, plus all the other humans and beings and forces that supported and encouraged this project and the detail collector.

ABOUT THE IMAGE-MAKER:
Corinne Teed is a research-based, multimedia artist working in printmaking, installation, time-based media and social practice. Their work lives at the intersections of queer theory, ecology, critical animal studies and settler colonialism. Teed currently teaches in the Art Department of University of Minnesota.

ABOUT THE DETAIL COLLECTOR:
the detail collector is a creative practice in the form of a blog where franciszka voeltz posts 1-10 details from the day nearly every day. in celebration of Vegetarian Alcoholic Press's fifth anniversary (which lands on August 8th), this chapbook is a collection of all the detail collector's August 8ths.
the detail collector is also a person named franciszka voeltz who writes poems to go on a portable typewriter for magnificent strangers and facilitates community writing events and workshops and serves as a faculty member at Thoreau College in Viroqua, Wisconsin.
more at franciszkavoeltz.com

SEP 2 4 2019

CPSIA information can be obtained
at www.ICGtesting.com
Printed in the USA
FSHW011855300719
60534FS